T0198982

Through the Reign of Rain

ROSEMARIE DRUCH

AuthorHouse™
1663 Liberty Drive
Bloomington, IN 47403
www.authorhouse.com
Phone: 1 (800) 839-8640

Published by AuthorHouse 02/22/2019

ISBN: 978-1-5462-4516-2 (sc)
ISBN: 978-1-5462-4517-9 (e)

Print information available on the last page.

This book is printed on acid-free paper.

authorHOUSE®

Ms. Rosemarie Druch is a professional poet, songwriter, and visual artist. She is also a musician, especially piano and some guitar and keyboard.

She was born in Philadelphia, PA. — where she was raised, studied, and still resides.

She is currently divorced.

Her daughter — Eva Marie — committed suicide in 1985, and she has a surviving son, Leon, a high school mathematics teacher.

She had taken all 4 years of creative writing in high school and published in her high school literary magazine.

She majored in English Literature at Temple University — main campus, Philadelphia, PA.

Later, when she was a substitute day care teacher with Federation Day Care Services at several sites in Northeast Philadelphia, PA., she took a number of formal visual arts courses, while working with the children of the nuclear accident in Chernobyl.

She also did other mediums on her own before and after these formal courses.

She has exhibited in 18 one-person shows and 10 group shows in Philadelphia and Bucks County, PA. since 1990.

She has 14 sets of poetry and art D.C. copyrighted, in the Library of Congress. All but "Seasons in Shadow" book of her poetry contain her art works.

This is her 6th collection to be published!

To all those who travelled with me through the years, especially since the Vietnam era, I dedicate this book to you!

"My Heart Quickens"

My Heart Quickens
With the light of day

Coming my way -
Maybe herein
As I go on to morning
Like
The 1st morning dew
For me and you...

And you
And you ...
Yes, without guess,
I feel the enlivening pain
Of beginning again,
As I write with my pen,
On the blank page...and
(For some)
Yet I still feel no rage!!
As I turn this page
Tonight
With moon bright!

"I yearn"

I yearn perhaps for sleep
But still I do not weep
Just silently, I go on
From Dust to Dawn,
Without a yawn.
I take you one more cup of coffee
As I start on again with my gifts:
To write, to play, to go' once more
To Yet another day
Its cool and wet outside
But warm within
With fireplace lights,
Before dawn,
On this side of the door
As is the spark of light inside me
to create endlessly!

"It's Like a Chain"

Some people complain,
Some talk such disdain
It's like a chain.
I stand with my cane
And
Go on again
Despite the return
Of the reign
Of rain.

"I don't feel much like Spring"

I don't feel much like Spring
This year
As tear upon tear
Fell from my eyes
Watering only
The flowers of my soul
To keep me whole!
Despite all that I despise
Around here!!..
Where I keep, as I weep,
All the creation
(of my being)
Songs, Poems & Paintings
Sacred near my heart
And
From which I never will part!!

"I wander"

I wander through the night
Of what's still wrong, not right
And fight with all my might
Not to take flight
But call to all
Who yet awake like me
To strike a bell for eternity
To beckon love
With the dove-

Always to be on the side of good and peace
That will move
And will never cease....
A fool not wise;
Not I!
With no disguise
I dry my eyes
The night is long
And so is my song
Of right and wrong
And
Though I tire and yearn for sleep
I shall not weep,
But the watch keep!

"Awakening"

Awakening
A few hours before early dawn
I ponder within and beyond
About this very day coming on.
I light a cigarette
And sit
Ready to begin again,
Not quit.
I hear the birds
Starting to sing
But not yet take wing,
As I question
What this day will bring!
Despite the might
Of the reign of rain,
I take up a pen
And write as then!

"While others sleep"

While others sleep
Through the night
I wonder, quiet, for the most part
As I pour one on paper, my heart,
And go not fast, not slow
Repairing for yet another show,
The glow of the moon dim,
Behind the clouds outside
As I, myself, try to hide
While the heavy rain falls harder
On the windowpane
And
The silhouette of the trees
With water blow
As do the flowers
And bushes below!
Alone my tears water my soul
While I let the feelings flow!

"Along the Road of Life"

Along the road of life
I met some who were nice
And some who were brutal
And took their told
That made me less than whole.

Yet on my journey this be
There were those who chose
The same path that I was on
And it's they who linger on to dawn!

The road has a heavy load
And is rough and tough
But I've made it through it all
And with will, not will, stand tall!

The flag waves but has a different meaning to me!
And forever waving it will be.

I've cried a million tears
But strove with cares and fears
To travel on, to who's beyond,
With heavy weight my shoulders thereon.
Still the muses those inspire me!

"Once again"

Once again
The reign of rain
Leaves
Pain
Severe
Out there –
Where puddles fill the street
In overburdening heat.
The stain of it is clear!!
More than just one tear
Has fallen down
Upon this weary old town,
With me in the midst
And misted -
Nor kissed, but wet all the way!
With dew
So drenched in sorrow
Until tomorrow.

"Far Beyond these Walls"

I wonder
And wander
Far beyond these walls
That surround me here
Where
No-one really cares
Yes, I have been elsewhere
Far and wide
Beside
The best of the races
And there's no conquest.
In Limbo
I await
A future date
With those
Whom I trust
And love -
Only there
The dove flies
Above the trees and the leaves.

"I See Far and Wide"

I see far and wide
And do abide
The road
That's long
With heavy load.
I reach out and about
To all along its path -
move
Without wrath...
My heart beats fast with memories
Of yesterday and today
As I go my way
And have my say,
And hear my song long today.

"Thirty Years"

Thirty years
Have passed away -
So many things
Happened in one year's disarray
But
I remember the whereabouts
And whens
So many tears, so much stress
I'll have to cry
It was quite a mess
And yet, through it all
Though disgust seem for all to...
In all the grief that stole
like a thief
There were some more proud moments though
As my son went through torture too–
Now I reach my hand out
To bridge the years
With all their fears
And go not with a grim part ...
I wonder too, with still a heavy heart,
If you and you and you
Recall it all too
In the mornings
Through morning's dew
And think of me
And think of him
When light glows bright
Not dim!

"There Will Be Love"

He is gentle and kind
And always on my mind.
His hug and kiss
I miss
When we're apart,
But he's forever
In my heart...
His voice soothes me
While on the phone,
When I'm alone,
And
Drives me on to dawn
And what's beyond!
Sometimes
I don't know what to say
As I go from day to day
But
Even without words
We can communicate,
Not berate or hate!!
And
As long as the dove
Flies above -
Though we've been through
A lot of pain
In the reign of rain -
There will be love!

"I Sit Here"

I sit here
With a cigarette in hand,
I haven't got a clue
And
I haven't got a plan -
But
I think of you and you
And
I try to understand
The night is closing in on me
With little sleep to go on
But
While I set my thoughts free
I set to works half-done
Through the darkness
to the dawn
First to pen, I go
Then to paint to show
and glow
And for this while
The muses three inspire me
As I go to my music true
- And do what I must do!

"Wandering"

Wandering in my mind –
Is life unkind?...
Is it fair
Out there
Where
Jokers are wild,
My child?
I ponder on this
As I throw a kiss
To those I miss!...
The weather's turned over and over again
With rain on rain
On my windowpane -
Yet, I travel on to dawn
And what's beyond
Before that fall
And that fall
And stood tall too
As I go on
To collect my due
For me and you
And you and you!!!!

"Despite the Reign of Rain"

Despite the reign of rain
Upon my windowpane
I have learned to love and live again
Oh! I feel his touch much
Upon me,
His voice soft and warm and low
His arms around me tenderly!...
Even though he's far away today
Yes I confess
Hour to hour
Like a flower
I grow
To show
And glow –
The sun is mine once again to shine
On this and that side of the door
Left for him, at least, ajar.

"I Sit Alone"

I sit alone now
Oh, somehow,
I've had my share of good times,
Friends, and loves, and lovers
In the past
And
Their memories will last –
Despite the tear and wear
Of year after year
Here
So I sit on a bench
In a different place
With no one's face
To see
That really matters to me
Anyhow
And later to music
Not muse
- And write another poem,
As I always will!!

"They'd never survive"

They'd never survive
All that I've been through
And it's the past
That keeps me alive –
Even in this surrounding
Negative present
They're not of my kind
- But, abound
They are...
And shallow
So, as I go on to my next dawn,
Within a yawn
I'll show
And glow
I still know my way
Into day
And
With will, not will,
Go or stay
And
Have my say!

"What I've Been Through"

What I've been through
And
What I'm still going through
Right now
Somehow
Is more than anyone
Should have to go through
I'm just trying
To collect my due..
I bear my scars
As if in wars –
And carry my wounds
(Old and new)
Within me true,
Near and far
Yes!
The tear from
The eye
Is never dry,
Though seldom seen
By others eye!..
No need to
Question why!!

"I still recall"

I still recall
As if it were yesterday..
No matter what some say
As I still bleed
The scar's still there –

This, from the wound
Will never end
My friend!
Yet

The rainbows
Dare
Come
Clear
Now
Somehow.

"Should I take the chance"

Should I take the chance
On another romance
And
Possibly get hurt again
And
Bring back here
The reign of rain
Upon my windowpane
Not much in common, true -
But, why feel blue?
And now, as many years pass,
I go —
Not slow.....

I travel a road
Meant just for few
Yes' travel I do
Where the grass
And the dew
Meet a rainbow far...
So, with the door ajar
I go
To such
Steadfast
With steps made to last -
Way beyond a lifetime
They
Now
Make me whole....

"Spring"

This is the beginning of spring
-And the reaffirming
Of who and what I am and stand for confirming
And all
On this and that side of the door
Sprouting out like seedlings
As the bell and the bells ring
To being once again
Despite the reign or rain
A beautiful flower
Hour to hour –
in a garden!...

I do not excuse your
Negativity
Through
Negativity
But
I will continue on
Dawn-to-dawn
With my productivity and creativity!

"Thirty Years Ago"

It's a Sunday Evening
In the beaming summer of the year clear
And though I'm tired
Not wired
As all
But
Stand tall
As bell and bells ring
I sing
A summer song
As I go along
My eyes hold back tears
For the last thirty plus years
The rain will fall again tomorrow
In sorrow
Just as did then
When
We last spoke —
No joke —
Oh!
The pain runs deep
Like a river
As I weep
Cut with a glass sliver!!

"As Long Ago"

As long ago,
Somewhere else
I sit on a bench
Somewhere,
Where I'm alone,
Far from my home
As I go to be shown
That I am
And be
On the ground
But a
Like a star
From afar
Twinkling
Mound to mound
For eternity –
Like the dove
High above,
As she flies
For peace
And
For love!

"Who the Hell Do You Think You Are?!"

Who the hell
Do you think you are?!
Degrading, accusing me!
You're the worst of all
But'
I stand tall
And
I wont fall!
I've known
Many insults —
Like you
And
I'm not taking it anymore
Stay on your side
Of the door!
I've been through
More
Than you can ever imagine
And
It did not destroy me,
And
I wont be destroyed now! -
Somehow!!

"Here"

Where Some Hide
Here
Is
And
Some abide

And
The brisk air
Enlivens me
Still,
Friskily,
On this autumn night
Without moon bright!

"I hear your voices"

Thirty Years and Fifty Years
Have gone by since then and when
With all their tears
And as yet, no fears
Of going on
To the dawn
And what's beyond
I hear your voices
Ringing through
And feel on eerie contact too
It's true
My heart still sings
Of you and you -
Your youth oh will always be
With me
Endlessly!!

"I Wander and Wonder"

I
Wander and wonder
In my mind
Is life unkind?..
Oh! No!! Beautiful it is to be
For those who go on fearlessly
Despite the stones
Along the way
I'll still find myself today
And stay
Not lonely, but alone
Sometime
With my rhymes!
Like
A Bell's
Chimes!!

"On This Ides of March"

On this Ides of March -
Beware
Out there,
Where
Tears on tears
Fall and
Call
I answer
Without a pout
And
Go
Without a shout!!...
Morning through mourning
Today
Seems far away
And
Yet
In dismay and disarray
I go on
Struggling towards the dawn!
Drizzling
Down
On
Me.

"By The Fireplace Light"

By the fireplace light
I write
Once more
On this side of the door
The air is pregnant with silence
As I do reminence –
A brief respite from pain
And rain upon the windowpane
While, with a smile,
I start again
Before dawn
Without a yawn!
Still the ivy grows
Before the snows ...
Leaves still on the ground,
All around!
My hand is steady
And I am ready
To fill the blank page,
Without rage
My thoughts play wild,
Like a little child,
As I go with the flow
And grow
And glow!!

"With Candlelights Bright"

With candlelights bright
I sit and write
Of wondrous things
And gossamers wings
The night envelope me softly
As I am free to be me
With no one around,
And from me not a sound!

My heart cries out over the years
And to these smiles despite the tears
My hands grasp tight the pen
As I remember the wheres and whens.

The music there inspire true
As I recall you and you and you
And the grandfather clock ticks
While the candle burns down its wick!

"The First Day of Spring"

It's the First Day of Spring
And I'm reaffirming
Who and what I stand for –
Sprouting out like a seedling
To become once again
A beautiful flowers
In life's garden..
I do not pardon you
For all the negativity,
But, will continue on
Dawn to dawn
With my productivity
And
Creativity
To soar
As before!
On this and that side
Of yet
Another
Door.

"With the muses three"

It's the onset of Spring
Yes, it is still Winter outside –
So, I hide inside
Where none can deride.

The tears are there,
Though none can see -
They're blind, deaf, and mute;
Their feelings dulled, not acute
So,
I keep hidden within
In time with my soul's rhythm –
With my songs, my poems, my heart
From which I'll never part.

I've been recorded published, shown
Awarded, certificated –
All on my own –
Taught too for a number of years,
All with my eyes full of tears.

Yes I've more still to do
Before I am through,
While my music will inspires me
With the muses three!!!

"I feel the fall of fall"

I feel the fall
Of fall once more
As I go out the dark
The drying leaves
Fall from the trees
With ease
As geese go flying south
I Call...
My sweater's on
At peak of dawn
As I go on
Without a yawn
And
The breeze
Does tease
While
Colors
Of the landscape wide---
DOT
Here and there—

As I escape the doldrums inside.

"I'm down Around Here"

I'm down
Around
Here
And
Bound
With
The
People
Not near but
With me always and in all ways
And
My tear
Is always in my eye
Though I try not to cry...
Why? Why?
Still I grow!
I've been through year's of cases
That it still carry about
In my dreams I'm back home
In my house, my dome
With my hat in my head
Like a crown
And my friends time,
And lovers too..
Here
I sit and stand and walk alone
Yes I intend to collect my due
Where my morning past mourning
Comes shining through!

"I wrote a long poem"

I wrote a long poem
Without end
As I recalled it all
Pass wall on wall
Yet stood tall,
And didn't and won't fall,

As long as the words
Soar like birds
On high
In the sky -
And
Though, yes, I still cry,
I'll always soar!
With the flag waving nearby
About right and wrong
I'll be strong!!
And noo
Nothing can find or blind me
For I see and be
Far and wide
And
I shall not hide!!

"What I Stand for"

Oh!
I've been abused
Used
Bruised
But
I'm still going strong
Despite
All the wrong –
And
In this city
Without pity
I go on to the dawn
To collect my due
For me and you and you!
As
The flag and the bell
Still tells well
Of the wishing well
Through all the hell!
Yes!
Right now, somehow,
I sit alone
In the early morning
Through all this mourning
On a bench
In a different place
That doesn't really know my face
And what I stand for
On this side of yet another door!!

"I Saw Your Smile"

Though in shadow —
I know —
I saw your smile tonight
And it lit up my heart...
Your gentle touch
I felt so light
And it warmed me inside
Where, lately, I hide
I trust your unending love
And fly with the dare.
Oh!
Now, somehow,
I doubt not my footsteps on the path I'm making
To tell and show
How high
The moon and stars
In the sky
As
I no longer ask 'Why?'.

Printed in the United States
By Bookmasters